HR SHARED SERVICES AND
THE REALIGNMMENT OF HR

Other titles from IES:

Employee Returns: Linking HR Performance Indicators to Business Strategy
  Carter A, Robinson D
  IES Report 365, 2000. ISBN 1-85184-295-0

The Fifties Revival
  Kodz J, Kersley B, Bates P
  IES Report 359, 1999. ISBN 1-85184-288-8

From People to Profits: The HR link in the service-profit chain
  Barber L, Hayday S, Bevan S
  IES Report 355, 1999. ISBN 1-85184-284-5

Attendance Management: a review of good practice
  Bevan S, Hayday S
  IES Report 353, 1998. ISBN 1-85184-282-9

Breaking the Long Hours Culture
  Kodz J, Kersley B, Strebler M T, O'Regan S
  IES Report 352, 1998. ISBN 1-85184-281-0

Keeping the Best: A Practical Guide to Retaining Key Employees
  Bevan S, Barber L, Robinson D
  IES Report 337, 1997. ISBN 1-85184-265-9

HR Information Systems: Stand and Deliver
  Robinson, D
  IES Report 335, 1997. ISBN 1-85184-261-6

From Admin to Strategy: the Changing Face of the HR Function
  Tamkin P, Barber L, Dench S
  IES Report 332, 1997. ISBN 1-85184-263-2

A catalogue of these and over 100 other titles is available from IES, or on the IES Website, www.employment-studies.co.uk

the *for* | **Institute**
Employment
Studies

HR Shared Services and the Realignment of HR

P Reilly

Report 368

Published by:

THE INSTITUTE FOR EMPLOYMENT STUDIES
Mantell Building
Falmer
Brighton BN1 9RF
UK

Tel.   + 44 (0) 1273 686751
Fax   + 44 (0) 1273 690430

http://www.employment-studies.co.uk

British Cataloguing-in-Publication Data

A catalogue record for this publication is available from the British Library

ISBN 1-85184-298-5

Printed and bound by Antony Rowe Ltd, Eastbourne

The Institute for Employment Studies

IES is an independent, international and apolitical centre of research and consultancy in human resource issues. It works closely with employers in the manufacturing, service and public sectors, government departments, agencies, professional and employee bodies, and foundations. For over 30 years the Institute has been a focus of knowledge and practical experience in employment and training policy, the operation of labour markets and human resource planning and development. IES is a not-for-profit organisation which has a multidisciplinary staff of over 50. IES expertise is available to all organisations through research, consultancy, publications and the Internet.

IES aims to help bring about sustainable improvements in employment policy and human resource management. IES achieves this by increasing the understanding and improving the practice of key decision makers in policy bodies and employing organisations.

The IES Research Club

This report is the product of a study supported by the IES Research Club, through which a group of IES Corporate Members finance, and often participate in, applied research on employment issues. The members of the Club are:

Anglian Water	Inland Revenue
BAA plc	Littlewoods Organisation plc
The Benefits Agency	Lloyds TSB Group
BOC Group	Marks & Spencer plc
BBC	NHS Management Executive
BT plc	Orange plc
Cabinet Office	Post Office
Corus Group plc	Rolls-Royce plc
Department of the Environment,	Scottish Equitable
Transport and the Regions	Scottish Executive
Glaxo Wellcome plc	Shell UK Ltd
Halifax plc	Smiths Industries plc
HM Customs & Excise	Standard Life
HM Prison Service	Unilever UK (Holdings) Ltd
Home Office	Woolwich plc

Acknowledgements

The author is indebted to participants of the research project and to Elaine Sheppard for her literature searches.

Contents

1. Introduction

1.1 The nature of the project

There is constant innovation in organisational structure. This applies as much to the HR function as to any other part of a business. Over the last few years there have been lots of changes in the way HR services have been delivered. In particular, many organisations have tried to devolve a number of personnel activities to line managers whilst at the same time trying to get a better alignment between the HR service and business needs. More recently, various organisations have chosen to concentrate their administrative personnel activities in what is frequently described as a centralised *shared service*. Sometimes this move is described as creating a *back office* function, where administrative processing is carried out separately from the main HR group. This is to be contrasted with front of house dealings with customers. Part of the shared service may be outsourced; alternatively, it may become part of a distinct organisational unit.

It is the creation of shared services or back offices that is the subject of this report. Views differ on the importance of this innovation in HR organisation. Some believe it to be of marginal interest, attested by the lack of examples. Anat Arkin, reporting in *People Management* (1999) on a survey of 153 organisations, wrote:

> 'The concept of shared services that appears so popular among certain multinationals seems to have barely surfaced in these (multi-site) organisations, with only four per cent planning to use them.'

The alternative position is that shared services is in the vanguard of fundamental change. Alf Turner, Director of HR UK Services at BOC, said at a recent conference:

> 'Separation of strategy from service delivery and the creation of shared services is in that league of change as the switch from welfare to personnel in the 1930s and from personnel to human resources in the 1980s.'

We cannot prove the truth of this contention, but this report will try to:

- understand the reasons why HR shared services are created
- discover their advantages and disadvantages in practice
- clarify the organisational choice between out- and in-sourcing the activity
- see whether HR has become more strategic as a result of introducing shared service.

Research to meet these objectives was supported by money from the IES Research Club. It was carried out by visiting 15 organisations in different sectors, most of which had introduced some form of HR shared service. Discussions with personnel teams covered the detail of how HR was structured, as well as the key research topics listed above. Direct feedback from customers of the shared service was not obtained, but HR interviewees were asked about how they gathered information on customer satisfaction, and what this had told them.

Less formally, the views and experience of organisations that had applied the shared services concept were obtained through attendance at conferences and other meetings. In addition, four consultancies were interviewed about their understanding of shared services, what they saw as its advantages and disadvantages, and where they thought the market was heading, especially with respect to outsourcing and technology developments.

Finally, a literature review was undertaken. This drew on material, especially from the United States, on how those with a longer track record of using shared services had fared.

1.2 What are HR shared services?

We will tend to use the term *shared services* in this report rather than 'back office function' because, as we discovered, not all that is carried out within a shared service activity is back office in nature. So what constitutes shared services? The key dimension of a shared service is, as the name implies, that the activities involved are those which are available to a number of parties. Moreover, the nature of the services is determined by both the provider and user. The significance of this is that, unlike traditional internal service provision, the customer defines the level of the service and decides which services to take up. Thus, as it has been more graphically put: *'the user is the chooser'* (Ulrich, 1995). A shared services model presupposes central provision. As we will see in Chapter 4, *shared* is not supposed to mean *centralised* in the traditional sense of that term, rather services are *common* to the recipients. There seem to be a variety of activities that can be included in shared services, not just administrative tasks. We will describe this point in more detail in Chapter 3.

1.3 The structure of the report

We will begin by looking at why shared services are introduced and what they involve. In Chapter 3.2 we will also consider how they were introduced. Chapter 4 looks at some of the issues in the delivery of shared services. The alleged benefits and disbenefits of operating in this way are covered in Chapter 5. The future of shared services is addressed in Chapter 6. Finally, in the last Chapter, we will examine the challenges that shared services face and consider the means to overcome any problems.

2. Why Create an HR Shared Service?

2.1 Overall picture

In our discussions with organisations, there were three principal drivers to the introduction of an HR shared service:

- cost
- quality
- organisational change.

Another factor in the equation was technology. In most of the circumstances we looked at, technology was usually a facilitator of change rather than a driver in itself. However, saying this may underestimate its impact. Some of the shared service models we examined would not have been possible only a few years ago. Technical innovation in communications has enabled far reaching structural change to take place.

These reasons were sometimes discrete, *eg* shared services were introduced primarily to save money; more often, the drivers were seen in combination. So a desire for cost saving and quality enhancement frequently both led to the introduction of shared services.

What was interesting given our previous work on outsourcing (Reilly and Tamkin, 1997), was that there was little evidence that the development of shared services was part of a reorganisation based on a core/periphery model. There was scarcely any suggestion that such a concept would determine whether an organisation would *make or buy* activities—concentrating on executing *core* activities itself, outsourcing the *peripheral* ones. As we will consider later, there was discussion about who should provide services, but this was more a debate about implementation than a question of fundamentals.

2.2 Cost reasons

Organisations felt that shared services could reduce costs by three main means:

1. by cutting staff numbers
2. by reducing accommodation charges
3. by greater efficiency in what was done and how it was done.

The first two benefits could be obtained by pulling together a number of separate administrative service activities into one place. This gave economies of scale and allowed the headcount to fall by some 20 to 40 per cent. This was done in one organisation by closing down regional support units in favour of a single, national centre. Another stripped out administrative work from business units and moved it to a cross-business office. Other organisations have worked from ratios of HR staff to total staff, or to revenue. They have discovered the industry average and sought to match or better it. This has given a target to aim for in what level of change is possible and, for some, desirable.

Besides saving on manpower, organisations could also reduce accommodation costs by exiting from several offices, or by cutting room space. Further reductions were sought by one or two of our case studies by re-locating the shared service centre to lower cost accommodation. Given that floor space apparently costs approximately £53 per square foot in central London compared with say £18 in Milton Keynes, there are obvious savings to be made in moving from high cost areas. However, the choice of location was generally more dictated by proximity to key customers than by finding the cheapest offices.

Organisations obtained greater efficiency in their administrative HR operations in a number of ways. It could be done by streamlining the services on offer. Creating shared services allowed organisations to confirm what it was that they should do, and what activities they should give up. Thus, where there was duplication of effort within parts of HR, and between HR and the line, tasks could be dispensed with. Ceasing to act *merely as a post office*, was the code often used to describe how nonessential activities were to be discontinued. Organisations often found that it was hard to get staff to drop work. Cutting numbers forced change on reluctant colleagues: they had no choice but to concentrate on key issues.

Having determined what to do, the next step was to simplify services and ensure that they were done to a high standard. We will cover this point further in the context of quality improvement, but there was evidence that financial savings could be made. By being clearer on service provision and standards, the aim was to reduce the amount of re-work that was done. The adage 'get it right first time' proved to be a money saver.

Economies of scale applied not just to headcount but also to service provision. ICL reported in the press an annual saving of £2 million through centralising recruitment services (Arkin, 1999). Such cost reduction can come from allowing only one or two central focal points to buy external services, such as recruitment advertising, car purchase, agency temps, or training. By using a restricted supplier list and offering the successful suppliers the high volumes of work that could come from company-wide coverage, meant that charges to the organisation could be slashed. ICL reported at a recent conference that placement fees had by these means been cut by over 40 per cent.

A final point to make about costs is that several respondents commented upon how the introduction of shared services made the expense of HR administration more transparent. Previously, such expenditure was buried in overheads without any true understanding of where money was being spent. HR staff might aim to get the work done with little awareness or interest in the cost. By identifying what needed to done, who was to do it and where, management was able to have a clearer picture of the cost of the service. Similar arguments have been advanced concerning project work. Having decisions on projects made in a more formal way meant that there was greater prioritisation of work than previously. Projects of limited value could be rejected, thereby saving on resources. Also, better management of projects would lead to better delivery in terms of time and money. Improving the quality of internal consultancy could mean less reliance on external consultancy — bringing real financial savings.

2.3 Quality reasons

A quite separate reason for introducing the shared services concept was identified as being to improve the quality of the HR delivery. This is closely tied to the need to enhance customer satisfaction. From the standpoint of quality development, there was a desire for the HR function to:

- be more professional in the work it did
- achieve greater consistency and accuracy
- be more aware of best practice internally and externally
- use better processes to complete its work
- deliver work on time and to budget.

All this, it was hoped, would give their customers an improved service. But more than that, it was felt that HR could strive for customer orientation in what they did, through:

- being consumer not producer driven, *ie* to think of what the customer wants rather than what suits the service supplier
- becoming more accessible, *eg* by opening HR services for longer hours or by easing the means of getting in contact
- improving the supply of information to customers, both on process and content
- giving better quality support in line with customer needs
- operating user-friendly services.

As we will see, technology facilitated a number of these changes, but it was felt to be more a change in attitude that was required. This was about how to find the best means to satisfy customer requirements, not necessarily by adopting the traditional means or the most convenient means. It suggests operating at a consistently higher standard and constantly seeking ways to improve. So in a sense there was an attempt to increase activity levels in the HR function as employers and line managers felt that services were more attuned to their needs and delivered in a way that was easy to deal with. As one respondent said: *'We are hoping to create friendly, non-threatening services which people also feel are non-judgmental.'*

2.4 Organisational reasons

There were four sorts of drivers to set up HR shared services that concerned organisational structure in some way.

2.4.1 Product of wholesale organisational change

In some instances, shared services came from HR participating in wider organisational change. This might be the result of devolvement of activities to line management necessitating a change in HR structure or, conversely, a re-centralisation, taking responsibilities away from devolved business units. Another type of alignment came with the introduction of a ubiquitous service culture within the organisation, of which HR was just part. So one company had gathered all its 'professional' services into a single division to support the operational side. The rules that HR adhered to were then those of the professional services division.

2.4.2 Achieving structural flexibility

Organisational reasons for change also derived from the belief that the shared service concept offered more structural flexibility. This meant it was easier for HR to support customers during business change — clients might re-configure their organisational structures, but a common support centre could easily adjust. More fundamental change, such as from a merger or acquisition, could also be accommodated.

2.4.3 Better organisational learning

This was not a prominent driver for change. The benefit to be obtained from cross-company learning was frequently more implicit than explicit. Nevertheless, organisations are concerned with knowledge management: how can the information distributed around the organisation be accessed for the good of everybody? By bringing services together in one place, there was the advantage that expertise was available for all, not just for a particular business. Good practice found in one operating unit might then be made available to the whole organisation. Information systems would be common, thereby improving access from different geographical parts of the organisation, across the various functional or business groupings and potentially for HR staff, line managers and, even, employees.

2.4.4 Re-positioning HR

Last but not least, there was the aim of re-positioning HR. One of the underpinning aspects of the creation of shared services in many organisations was the desire to change the role of HR. This universally meant trying to help the function become more strategic and less bogged down in administrative activities. The root cause of this desire for re-alignment is that for many years the function has suffered an identity crisis. It has not been sure of its role and has doubted the contribution it can make to the business. It has experienced problems from *'ambiguity, marginality, the ivory tower syndrome and being labelled as the organisational policeman'* (Torrington, 1998). These feelings have been exacerbated by some business leaders rubbishing the work of HR and questioning the quality of the people who are recruited to or transferred into the function. As Ulrich (1998b) has put it: HR departments are too often *'like computers made up of used parts'* — a reference to the fact that many HR departments have had foisted on them people who could not 'hack it' elsewhere.

Further pressure on the function has arisen from the environment within which HR has been operating. Over much of the 1980s and 1990s, industrial relations have become steadily more stable. The power of trade unions has been eroded through declining membership and de-recognition. The reduction in importance of IR has simultaneously weakened the power of the Personnel function. Personnel staff gained much authority from their ability to manage the collective bargaining process and handle dealings with the unions. Instead, in a largely slack labour market, management asserted its power and marginalised HR's role to facilitating downsizing. As research (Purcell and Ahlstrand, 1994; Connolly *et al.*, 1997 and Lecky-Thompson, 1997) suggests, HR has had little say in influencing business strategy, but it has suffered the opprobrium (from employees) of executing the decisions that have flowed from it.

The arrival of the Human Resource Management philosophy has in some senses added to the function's difficulties. Whilst many personnel departments happily renamed themselves human resources, the HRM movement stressed the importance of the line manager interacting directly with individual employees, and taking responsibility for their management. People issues are seen as too important to leave to the HR department. This view has pushed the function towards devolution, but questioned what its role should be.

So the aim of HR has been to move from:

- a short-term to long-term orientation
- a purely operational to a more strategic role
- a reactive tendency to a more proactive orientation
- a policeman of rules to an advisor to the line
- an upholder of tradition to a facilitator of change
- an employee welfare service to a business support function.

In other words, HR is seeking to avoid a low profile, fire-fighting role and seeking to become an explicit, high profile contributor at the strategic level, well integrated with the business and demonstrably adding value. HR should then be *'acting as a catalyst for change … anticipating problems and making events happen'* (Hutchinson and Wood, 1995).

We have tried to capture these changes graphically. Figure 1 indicates how the emphasis many within the function would like to see, shifts from a short-term administrative role to one with a longer-term strategic emphasis. This change is often represented

Figure 1: Development of the HR role

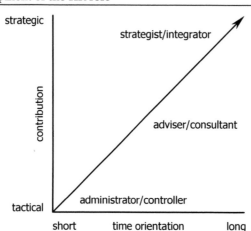

Source: IES

The Institute for Employment Studies

by altering the shape of the HR delivery—from pyramid to diamond, as the administrative activity is pared from the base of the pyramid.

To achieve these objectives, besides re-stating HR's role, some organisations have attempted a concomitant devolution of personnel activities to line managers and a move towards a self help culture for employees. Both managers and staff are expected to do more for themselves than in the past, and rely less on HR. So, a move to shared services may be intended to assist a change in the positioning of HR, but to be successful it may have to be accompanied by other initiatives. We will return to this subject in Chapter 4.

2.5 Technological facilitation

Where technology has directly led change, it occurred because of the purchase of a new company-wide computer platform or a new HR Information System. Either of these developments offered fresh possibilities in what could be achieved by data manipulation, or required a re-think of how HR services were delivered. In the latter case, this arose because the cost/benefit justification for new kit might well have been predicated on headcount savings that could only come from the centralisation of services. A common IT base also allowed the networking of information that permitted service innovation.

Technology as an enabler of change was a common feature in the introduction of shared services. It came from using such things as:

- an organisational intranet to provide information on HR policies and procedures. This meant that the organisation has only 'one version of the truth', not the variety of different paper based versions.

- PIN number based access to personal information, *eg* on options to flex individual reward packages

- sophisticated telephony such as IVR (interactive voice response) to offer callers a choice of options to key into from a voice menu, or distributed call systems allowing callers to be routed to remote locations

- document management systems, *eg* allowing paper to be scanned so as to feed electronic files, to transfer material electronically, and to permit multiple access by HR staff

- work flow systems that guide and prompt the user as to the next steps to be taken
- standard forms on the intranet that could be electronically completed and despatched to an administrative centre so that re-keying could be avoided.

2.6 Summary

To give an illustration of the contrasting drivers for change, set out below are two different contexts within which shared services were introduced.

In one organisation, quality improvement was the rationale:

HR was seen as:

- adding insufficient value to the business
- too bureaucratic/fragmented
- inefficient and inconsistent.

HR needed to:

- get the basics right
- focus on what was important
- understand what managers required.

In another organisation, cost reduction was the principal reason.

The aim of the re-organisation in HR was to:

- respond to wider organisational change
- substantially reduce the costs of delivering HR services
- challenge how HR added value to business
- achieve ratios of HR staffing to total manpower that were at least as good as competitors.

To achieve these objectives:

- headcount was to be reduced
- the HR structure would be re-configured
- administrative processes would become more efficient
- clearer line accountabilities for personnel activities would be set
- greater self administration by employees would be required
- HR would become more business driven in its role.

These examples illustrate that though there may be primary drivers to launching shared services, there are often secondary benefits that organisations are hoping to realise. So cost savings may be the primary reason for change, but, at the same time, improving quality may also be seen as an important objective.

3. What are HR Shared Services and How Were They Introduced?

3.1 What does HR shared services involve?

There was, in fact, no single model of shared services in our study. If you consider Figure 2, organisations commonly distinguish between strategic, operational and administrative activities. Strategic work was always excluded from shared services, as it was seen as a corporate responsibility. How broadly the term 'strategic' was conceived, however, varied greatly. A governance function was always included, with a broad policy direction. This meant ensuring that the organisation met certain standards and followed the same broad approach to people management. Such things as values, mission, vision and objectives were typically seen as part of the corporate domain.

Figure 2: HR organisation: broad choices

Strategic	policy
	governance
Operational	centres of excellence
	relationship management
	project work
	consultancy
Support	information and advice
	administrative
	record keeping

Source: IES

Senior management issues (pay and succession) might also be reserved for the corporate centre, along with external affairs. Other companies have additional corporate priorities: ABB reportedly emphasise the corporate contribution to international resourcing, whilst GEC believe in the protection and promotion of core, organisational competencies (Connolly, *et al.*, 1997). In one of our cases, policy development was not part of the corporate responsibility. This was because the organisation wished to keep corporate overheads to a minimum. It was internal politics rather than service optimisation that determined the structure. In other organisations, there was a more conventional division between policy determination at the centre and execution at operational level.

At the other end of the spectrum, administrative tasks were, not surprisingly, the bread and butter of the shared services function. Items forming part of the service included:

- payroll changes (on/off/variation)
- relocation services
- recruitment administration
- benefits administration (including flexible systems and share schemes)
- company car provision
- pensions administration
- employee welfare support
- training support
- absence monitoring
- management information.

Not all these services were included in every shared service centre we saw. Some (*eg* relocation services) were outsourced. Others as a matter of choice were excluded. One organisation took recruitment administration out of shared services because the high volume, short deadlines of recruitment did not fit with the less intensive payroll/record changes work.

The greatest difficulty occurred in defining the boundaries of shared services was not at either of the extremities of Figure 2, but in the operational middle. Here there was a great deal of variation in what was included. All of our organisations had an HR person in a customer facing role, variously described as business partner or adviser, or relationship manager. They either reported to a line manager or to a senior HR manager, usually, but not always, separately from the shared services organisation. This individual, or at most small team, was expected to support their line clients in terms of strategic development, organisational design and change management. This added up, in the words of one company, to 'transformational' activities, to be contrasted with transactional services. Administrative services in support of these HR managers were, of course, provided from the shared service centre.

In many of our case study organisations, further support to HR or line customers came from one or all of the following:

- an intranet to give details of personnel policies and procedures
- a telephone customer helpline to advise on the interpretation of these policy and procedures
- a project or consultancy pool of advisers able to tackle longer-term problems
- centres of excellence with expertise in such areas as resourcing, employee relations, reward or training.

All of these activities were found in the shared services centre, but some were, again, organisationally discrete. Some services (helpline or intranet) provided the line manager with information such that there was no need to bother their HR business partner with trivia or simple issues. The centres of excellence or consultancy pool gave assistance over a more extended period, and with more professional help. In some organisations, guidance was provided to line managers directly; in others, these services were accessible by HR alone, which contracted or used them on behalf of their business partner.

Services centres mostly provided information or advice to individual employees. Helplines or intranets were there for their use as much as for line managers. Other organisations restricted their helplines to supporting managers. Employees might instead be able to access external counselling services. Certainly, in all our organisations, employees were not expected to trouble the HR business partner with day to day operational issues – this would divert them from concentrating on strategic issues.

The complex reporting relationships and nature of centralisation and devolution is captured in Figure 3.

Figure 3: HR organisational models

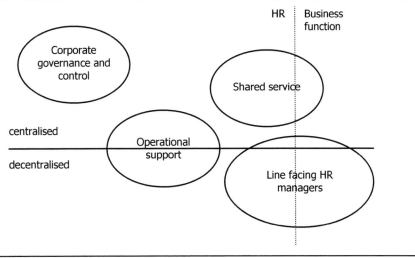

Source: IES

Figure 4: A typical HR organisation with shared services

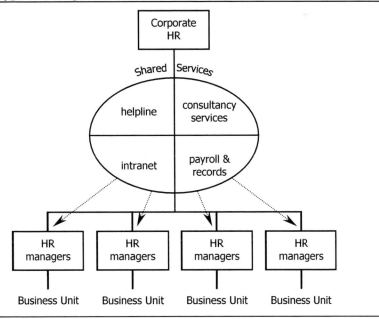

Source: IES

This illustrates that in relation to the two dimensions of centralised/decentralised and HR/business located, there are many models in operation. HR corporate governance is naturally only located centrally within the function. But shared services can be found in the business or HR organisation, though always centrally placed. HR operational support may be centrally provided or not. Business partners may report to HR or the line, and are usually located close to business units.

Figure 4, however, gives an idealised picture of the most typical structure we found.

3.2 Form of introduction

In simple terms, the way in which shared services came about reflected the driver for its introduction. So in some companies it was part of a wider organisational change, *eg* to cut costs or construct a common shared services model. In other cases, there was a narrower re-structuring or re-positioning of the HR function itself, driven by the HR team. Here the impetus was frequently the HR director's own dissatisfaction with the nature of the HR offering, rather than a need to respond to an organisational pressure from outside the function.

Some organisations made their changes without the help of external consultants; others relied on outsiders either for diagnosis or design, or both. Diagnosis involved such things as:

- establishing what the different parts of HR did
- determining the process connections in activities
- establishing customer views of the worth of HR services
- assessing the skills of members of the HR team.

Design included re-configuring the structure of the function, producing new policy and procedure manuals or putting together the technological elements — call centres, intranets, *etc.*

The extent of line involvement in the creation of shared services varied. Some line managers participated in the conceptualisation, design and implementation of shared services. Others were consulted, but did not otherwise contribute. A common view of those managers responsible for the introduction of shared services is that insufficient time was devoted to bringing line managers on board. Either they were consulted too late, or in insufficient detail. Likewise, there was a feeling that HR staff themselves may not always have been handled correctly. Several people remarked that HR staff were the most resistant to change and thus they needed the most convincing. The learning point for those involved was that organisations needed to communicate, communicate and communicate.

We have already observed that downsizing was a characteristic element in the introduction of shared services. Besides altering the quantum of the function, there was also in many cases a change sought in the contribution of individual staff. The skills that would be required in the new organisation were not the same as those needed in the old structure. Some incumbents did not like the different style of work, and took the opportunity to move on. In a few organisations, HR Managers were changed because they remained unconvinced of the value of shared services. New staff were recruited or assigned from elsewhere in the organisation as replacements. There was a common pattern of bringing in people with customer skills, but not necessarily a personnel background, in place of those with technical know-how. It was felt that the latter could be learnt, but that the right sort of attitude was harder to pick up on the job. Telephone and PC skills were also seen as vital. As one respondent put it: *'your keyboard is your pen'*.

If physical relocation accompanied the introduction of shared services, the need for recruitment was likely to be greater. In most of the cases we covered, shared services were sited at an existing location at least initially. Where there was a later transfer to a new site, a whole new team was recruited afresh.

The box below shows how one company went about the introduction of shared services in a thoroughgoing manner.

> One organisation began by defining the activities to be undertaken. Next it described the capabilities required to complete these tasks, and then it examined the capabilities of its existing employees to see how far they matched. On this basis, people were selected for their posts and transfers in or out were determined to manage the surplus/shortfall. External recruitment was used where there was insufficient internal resource. Capability gaps also led to a programme of training.

Without perhaps being as systematic as the example above, all the case study organisations had invested in training. This was both in knowledge training, *eg* how the maternity policy worked, and skills training, *eg* how to deal with a stroppy customer. Some of the training was very informal, *eg* lunchtime seminars; in other cases external expertise was used.

Where the introduction of shared services required a switch of responsibilities from HR to the line, there was, at minimum, a need to inform managers about their new tasks. In some organisations this went further in terms of knowledge and skills training, *eg* how to conduct a recruitment interview without breaching equal opportunities legislation.

One organisation took the view that it was best to push their managers in at the deep end; in other words, not to spend much time preparing them for their new responsibilities but to find out the consequences afterwards. Training could then be targeted on real needs, not based on anticipated fears. Other research suggests that line managers may feel that experience is more important than training, in learning how to deal with HR issues (Cunningham and Hyman, 1999). This may reflect the gifted amateur approach of too much UK management — you pick it up as you go along — or a view of the relative unimportance attached to people management issues. Instead, it may simply be a reflection of limited time available to improve skills and knowledge. As one manager talking of devolvement said: *'We're working at such a pace that training doesn't get done properly'* (Hutchinson and Wood, 1995).

4. Issues in How Shared Services are Delivered

4.1 Centralisation

A characteristic of shared services is that they provide a central resource. Through this means, cost savings are achieved by economies of scale and greater consistency of approach. Centralisation in this way goes against the grain of what many organisations have been doing in pushing power away from the centre, closer to the operational action.

However, as with HR planning (Reilly, 1996), organisations have discovered that there are costs to decentralisation that they would rather avoid, especially the cost of supporting diversity and innovation. Illustrations of this could be seen in the multiple reward or performance management systems across a company, often as variations on a theme. One organisation, for example, discovered it had six competency based pay schemes covering six different business units, each broadly similar, but with subtle variations. BOC found that they also had six HR information systems 'none of which talked to the others—or to payroll' (Turner, 2000). All could be justified in meeting the particular needs of their business, but whether these advantages were sufficient to justify the additional costs was doubted. Organisations could, moreover, see benefits in pulling activities together in terms of commonality of information capture and learning. However, corporate offices do not now regard a centralised command and control model as appropriate, in current circumstances where organisations must be fleet of foot in response to customers or competitors. What organisations are usually looking for is the best of both worlds: operational responsiveness within a corporate framework. They wish to avoid the criticisms of the past that corporate HR foisted on business units best practice HR models (*eg* of performance management, reward or management development) irrespective of whether these met their operational needs. There was no choice but to accept these policies and little chance to customise them to suit local circumstances.

The essence of shared services is that it offers not just a common delivery, but one which meets the customer's needs rather than those of the corporate centre. So it is not true centralisation. Ulrich (1995) explains it thus:

> *'Shared services is not the rebirth of centralization. In fact, while it may look like centralization, it is just the opposite. In a centralized organization, corporate controls the resources and dictates policies, programs and procedures to the field. In a shared services organization, resources from the field are shared, but the control over the use of these resources resides with the field.'*

An American manager talks of the difference as between 'standardization' of services which occurs in a central model, compared with 'optimization' of services for customers as found in the shared services concept (McWilliams, 1996).

The central structures, we saw, were balanced by having HR managers close to the customers, so that there were elements of a decentralised service too. Also, whilst resources were centrally organised, there was scope for tailored advice, policy or practice to suit individual business unit needs. Yet, given that the same people may be providing guidance on reward, there was likely to be a fair degree of similarity across the organisation. Differences, it would be hoped, would be the product of real variations in business circumstance, not a reflection of the prejudices of a particular HR manager.

The aim must be as Sydney Lentz (1996) found in his study of shared services, that the successful organisations: *'managed to integrate the competitive features of customer focus and flexibility with the equally competitive features of economies of scale'*. This produces what he calls 'hybrid' structures, where the organisation: *'decentralizes decision making to the operating units and centralizes administrative functions to the corporate staffs'*.

4.2 Devolution

Decentralisation and devolvement tend to go hand in hand, though not always. The desire to limit the power of the corporate centre over policies and procedures, which leaves little discretion to operational personnel units, is frequently seen as consistent with the aim to maximise line manager responsibilities for people management.

There has been a general trend for activities to be transferred from personnel to line managers that has been going on for some time. This has been primarily motivated by a desire to increase local accountability, but also to speed decision making (Industrial Relations Services, 1994). In a number of the change programmes of our case study organisations, this has been a vital element in the re-positioning of HR, getting way from its 'nanny' role to higher value added activities. It has also seemed to be necessary in some organisations as the numbers in the HR department have dwindled (Hall and Torrington, 1998).

However, one organisation interviewed took a contrary view, accepting that line managers wanted to get on with their principal tasks and not be diverted by minor 'irritations'. In this organisation it was accepted that HR provided the role as an 'intelligent agent' guiding staff and managers through the maze of complex policy. They wished to avoid the reaction reported in other case study organisations, that HR is all too keen to push issues back to the line or give them 'take it or leave it' advice (Cunningham and Hyman, 1999).

In practice, what is devolved varies greatly — is it activities (doing things) or responsibilities (being accountable for things)? Perhaps just as important, what devolution actually means can be quite different from organisation to organisation, or from topic to topic. Thus research by Torrington (1998) suggests that on some subjects it is more common for management to develop strategy without HR participation (especially work design), whereas on others HR may take a stronger lead (*eg* recruitment). However, on the vast majority of subjects there is a clear line/HR partnership at work (namely, on HR planning, performance management, training management development, career management, employee relations and reward). At an operational level, it seems that responsibility has been passed to line managers across a broad spectrum of activities, especially recruitment and selection, employee relations, performance management and work organisation, but that again a partnership approach appears to be the most common model (Hall and Torrington, 1998). There is evidence, though, from the Hall and Torrington research that full devolvement has only occurred in relation to routine administration (*eg* the recording holidays or sickness), and the direct people management (*eg* discipline or welfare). Moving such activity to the line is hardly radical, and indeed in many organisations never really formed part of HR's role in the first place.

Nevertheless, devolution has not, it seems, been without problems. While some managers have welcomed their increased freedom to act, others have floundered, requiring HR staff to come to bail them out. Difficulties from the managerial perspective seem to centre on a lack of time or skills to undertake new work. This might include being unaware of the limits of their authority. From a corporate standpoint, there has been concern about a lack of consistency across the organisation in people management, with some unjustifiable differences in employee treatment emerging. There has also been resistance from personnel staff to losing control over activities that were once seen to be under their aegis. Those organisations that had taken the process gradually and given managers plenty of support, through training, helplines or written guidelines, seem to have adapted best to the devolutionary process.

4.3 Insourcing or outsourcing

Some shared services have been located in the body of the HR function. Sometimes this is formally part of the corporate centre, sometimes it is a separate department within HR, and sometimes it is loosely connected to the corporate centre with strong links to the business units. In other organisations, shared service centres have formed part of a professional services arm. Here there is often a separate organisation within the company as a whole. Going further than this, some have badged their shared service as a discrete entity, at arm's length from the rest of the organisation. This may be the precursor to operational independence, where it goes from being a budget cost centre to a profit centre, expected to generate its own income to cover its costs. The London borough of Hackney has set up its personnel services team (called the HR consultancy unit) as one of 19 trading units operating within the Council. Each is independent in financial terms, makes its own decisions and raises revenue for selling services (Industrial Relations Services, 1998). None of the case study organisations had as yet offered services externally, but one is on the point of so doing.

None of the organisations had outsourced the whole of their shared service operation, nor seemed likely to do so in the immediate future. However, some organisations explicitly recognised that by being clear as to their costs, this allowed easier external comparisons to be made. Benchmarking information could then be used not only to pare down internal costs, but also to challenge whether the service could be performed more cheaply externally.

Particular parts of the HR service had been outsourced amongst our organisations. These included some or all of the following services:

- payroll
- training
- recruitment
- pensions administration
- benefits administration.

These activities are easily ring fenced and capable of being allocated to another organisation to perform on the client's behalf. One company had gone a step further in outsourcing its helpline and induction and exit processes.

Outsourcing was favoured where there were high investment costs (time and money), especially with respect to new technology, or where there was a high volume of routine activities. Staff turnover and an inability to recruit suitable staff was another contributory factor. Clearly there also had to be a service provider with the capability of handling the work. This had initially discouraged some companies from pursuing outsourcing. Press reports of substantial, if only partial, outsourcing (*eg* Westminster City Council's £2 million deal with Capita to provide personnel support and administrative services, or BP Amoco's £370 million contract for Exult to perform its administrative data handling) may remove this concern.

4.4 Structuring the service

Most of our organisations had decided on creating generalists in an administrative part of their shared service centres, but with some specialist support. In other words, within their area of responsibility, HR staff covered a range of activities as generalists, but with expertise provided (say, in pensions administration) in specific areas. A minority of organisations preferred specialisation. This meant that all staff handled a narrow range of administrative work.

In the other areas of the shared service centre, *eg* the consultancy or project pool, there were similar differences to be found. Again the preference was towards creating generalists capable of handling a wide variety of work, but once more recognising that there were areas of specialism that needed to be performed by experts. However, there was the view expressed that creating specialists helped because there was a concentration of expertise to tackle issues in depth, rather than superficially in the way that happened in traditional structures.

One method of balancing the generalism/specialism tension was to ask employees to be all-rounders, but expect them to develop an expertise in one subject. Thus project consultants might be capable of tackling any issue, but each might specialise in handling a particular case, be it to do with resourcing or training. Similarly, administrative assistants might do all kinds of work but develop a deeper knowledge on say managing share option benefits.

The approach adopted depended in part on whether there were centres of excellence, where they were located, and how they were staffed. If they formed part of the shared services centre and were resourced by genuine experts, then a generalist approach to consultancy was more likely to be successful.

Table 1 illustrates what the distinction between generalism and specialisation might look like in practice.

The benefits and disbenefits of creating generalists and specialists should be obvious. Having the former gives more resource flexibility in being able to balance work demands with the staff available. In individual development terms, employees can grow a wide knowledge of subject areas. Its disadvantage is that

Table 1 : Generalist or specialist roles in shared service centres

Area of activity	Generalist role	Specialist role
Administrative services	all forms of record/payroll changes	distinction between those who handled payroll changes from other records
	management of all forms of cases, *eg* sickness, maternity	experts in maternity, sickness absence *etc.*
	administration of various benefit schemes, *eg* health insurance	specialists in car fleet management, recruitment support, *etc.*
Consultancy/project support	tackles any form of project for any client	alignment with specific businesses covering their problems only or work on issues only within specific subject area (*eg* reward or development)
Helplines or other means of information or advice	rotation of staff between activities, *ie* manning the help desk one day, then doing detailed casework the next and working on improving information on the intranet on the day following	concentration on particular methods of support. So working exclusively on the phone, doing intensive casework or improving published procedures

Source: IES

people become jacks of all trades and masters of none. Specialisation, by comparison, avoids the problem of spreading knowledge too thinly, but risks staff complaints that work is too repetitive. The answer, as some of our organisations found, was that some work, especially administrative, needs variety to make it palatable, and those that have over-specialised have discovered staff dissatisfaction. Similarly, some tasks have to be done on a rotational basis, *eg* telephone helplines, to avoid over-stressing staff. Other areas of work are too complex, *eg* managing pensions administration, to be done by anyone other than someone specifically trained. The hope is that the work is rich enough to prevent boredom.

Another area of debate concerns how the shared services are physically delivered. One view was that technology enabled the service to be executed by people who are widely dispersed, even when completing the same function. Thus, for example, payroll entries could be made at a number of different sites. This is then a *virtual* shared service centre, with a common management structure but distributed execution.

The alternative position is that, whilst technologically possible to deliver services from a number of physical centres, this defeats a large part of the logic of having *shared* services. Pulling them together gives the opportunity for optimum resourcing that is more difficult to achieve without co-location. Also, the latter helps develop an esprit de corps that should generate common and improved service standards. Having staff all in one place allows such techniques as *buddying*, which helps with cover and improved learning. One organisation used the fact that staff were located together to get subject specialists to spend a period of time each month on the helpline to get a better understanding of what pressures their colleagues were under. This helped them when calls were referred to them for specialist advice.

An added argument in favour of co-location comes when a team moves into new office space. It was argued by some of our interviewees that this can help both practically (in having custom designed facilities) and psychologically (demonstrating change and creating improved work relationships).

This argument is more forceful when discussing a particular type of service — helpline, administrative processing or project support. However, some extend the benefits of co-location to combine different services in the same place. There are several arguments advanced in favour of this position:

- cross-group learning and information flow is better
- escalating problems to a higher level of expertise is easier
- boundary management of problems is less common
- for developmental or operational reasons, people can be transferred without difficulty to other work areas.

4.5 Service definition and monitoring

One of the advantages of the shared services model is that it allows service provision to be more closely defined. This is both in relation to customers and internal performance. Thus organisations have put in place quality control measures to ensure that output is to the requisite level. This has in part been achieved by laying down standard procedures, supported by performance metrics. This enables the organisation to determine how quickly, for example, an offer letter, processed after an interview or a promotion, can be generated. Results can then be tracked. For more complicated processes, such as supporting a maternity case, systems can flag when action is required, thereby reducing the chances of error by omission.

Monitoring can, and in some case study organisations does, go beyond merely measuring performance to fault finding. More than in the past, errors are likely to be visible and not easily suppressed. One organisation was working hard to get acceptance from its shared services team that identifying mistakes, owning up to them and then finding ways of rectifying them was a positive matter. It meant that estimating the cost of re-work was now transparent, and with effective action taken, efficiency savings could be measured.

Delivering a quality service is also likely to be enhanced by internal control procedures that ensure that people know their area of expertise, and do not go beyond their capability. This was expressed in several organisations in having *escalation* procedures. This means that if, for example, a call comes in to the helpline asking for information, it can be dealt with by the service operator, but if the caller then starts asking for interpretation of policy, then the operator is required to pass the caller to a policy specialist. To give an idea of the difference: at IBM's Ask HR, the average routine phone call is dealt with in two minutes, whilst the target time for a more complex question passed to a specialist is two days (Industrial Relations Services, 1999a).

One organisation had the following levels of service:

1. Information management
2. Case management
3. Advisory service
4. Specialist support.

At level 1, informants were given basic information, say, about terms and conditions of employment or company procedures. Cases would be referred to level 2 if they required more time or a degree of interpretation. If they were more complicated still, because of policy complexity or the unique circumstances, then an advisory service would be used. Finally, specialist expertise in, say, reward or resourcing would tackle issues which were more to do with policy changes.

Monitoring was done in our organisations by how well services were delivered in terms of timeliness or accuracy. Some extended monitoring to 'cases', *ie* problems under investigation. Information gathered through phone calls or face to face discussion was logged, along with actions taken. This gave a record of the case for the files, essential if ever there were to be disciplinary or legal consequences. It also allowed management to see patterns—*eg* an increase in bullying cases, or a rise in disputes within a particular department.

Some case study organisations had used their growing capacity to monitor performance to create Service Level Agreements (SLAs) between HR and its customers. These 'contracts' usually specified the services offered, their frequency and the quality standards to be expected. Some companies have gone further and attached a monetary value to the services. This might be through a block charge per SLA (*eg* based on customer head count) or itemised billing for services as used (*eg* per training course).

There was a debate on the benefits of having formal SLAs with a monetary element, compared with informal systems. Proponents of SLAs argued that formalising the services offered and defining quality standards, made for less ambiguity in expectations. Having a monetary element, it was argued, meant that the debate over services was taken seriously. The more commercial orientation of HR might be designed to fit a more commercial attitude in the business more generally. HR is then using terms and techniques familiar to their line customers and ones which give credibility to the HR offering. Clients were more particular in what they sought; suppliers knew that the services offered were needed. It also gave staff real targets at which to aim.

The contrary argument was that, as one interviewee put it: '*you create an industry in itself*'.

In other words, the monitoring process generates such activity that the point of the exercise, the substantive content of the work, takes second place to the process of measuring it. Less controversially, others argued that either there was not a culture of SLAs within their organisation—so creating one would be a radical step—or that the financial systems did not permit proper service costing. Indeed, those organisations with *activity based costing* clearly have an advantage compared with those whose financial systems are less sophisticated. Amoco shared services in the USA apparently undercharged its customers by a mere $100 million dollars because it failed to get its pricing structure right (McWilliams, 1996).

Besides monitoring performance metrics internally, some organisations engaged in undertaking customer satisfaction checks. Questionnaires are often used to establish views on quality, timeliness and cost of the service. Random phone calls to users are also common. Some organisations have customer panels to agree service provision and monitor outcomes. Intranets may have an email return facility to generate feedback on the content and layout of intranet pages. Alternatively, there may be specific pages on the intranet to allow comments to be made.

Where possible, organisations have benchmarked their service provision against external markers. This has been especially useful when comparing delivery costs with those of other organisations.

Monitoring performance has another benefit. Seeing how well the function performs can demonstrate to sceptical management its reliability, efficiency, *etc*. This may be important if the HR department is arguing for more resources or trying to protect itself from manpower cuts. Rather like the train performance indicators, if you have a high proportion of activities completed on time, it helps protect against criticism for the odd service failure.

Monitoring is helpful but of limited value unless organisations learn from the results, especially where there have been problems. Too many projects have been implemented without proper review. Several organisations which have introduced shared services intend to audit their operation after a year or so's operation; others have not yet seen the need to do so. Lack of follow-up has been seen in other research: only six out of 24 organisations had consulted managers about devolution after implementation (Industrial Relations Services, 1994) in a process that was not without its problems. Whilst regular monitoring picks up service deficiencies in timeliness, quality or cost, some service failures may not be registered. What if potential users are bypassing HR services? For example, a line manager dissatisfied with recruitment through HR goes out and hires his own staff; or worse. In one case study organisation, such was the desire of a senior manager to control all his activities, he created his own internal personnel structure. This was in the days before shared services and had more to do with the megalomania of the particular manager than any comment on the quality of the HR department. But dissatisfied customers, for what ever reason, will solve their own problems by declaring UDI.

5. The Benefits and Disbenefits of HR Shared Services

5.1 Advantages of shared services

As one might expect, the benefits of shared services are the ones sought by organisations when they introduced their new structures; namely:

- lower costs, both in terms of numbers employed and accommodation required

- more efficient resourcing, within a bigger shared service centre pool than is possible if staff are distributed across a number of teams

- better quality of service, more consistent delivery to a higher, common standard. Non-compliance is more easily exposed.

- customer satisfaction ratings increased, especially relating to those staff selected for their interpersonal skills

- improved match between customer expectations and service delivery, through more explicit contracting

- a single point of contact, making it easier for customers to access the HR function

- allows more of an integrated 'total solution' approach to a problem, rather than one fragmented by involvement of different HR disciplines

- greater transparency of costs makes decisions on services better informed and more commercial

- HR is more selective in what it does, so that it can have a greater impact. Time is given to issues of more strategic importance.

- better project management—delivery more likely to be on time and to specification

- HR consultants can develop a wider expertise in covering a range of issues

- career development is facilitated by being able to rotate staff through different service streams

- cross-group learning within the shared service centre can be augmented

- development of a cross-organisation common information base, accessible to all

- better management information, provided more consistently across the organisation as a whole

- facilitating corporate investment, especially in computing and communications infrastructure, where a bigger entity, like a shared service centre, can command resources in a way that smaller units cannot.

5.2 Disadvantages of the shared services model

As the case study organisations were generally positive about their experiences, there were few problems identified. There were some difficulties encountered, either in implementation or in the running of the shared service operation. These were:

- neglecting the importance of the knowledge and experience of those who had performed administrative roles in the past. They had the technical expertise in HR policies and procedures. They had established good relationships with customers based on knowing the people and the culture. Ignoring this factor in resourcing shared service centre posts had led to a deterioration in the quality of services.

- the risk of de-skilling some administrative jobs to the point where they become extremely tedious to do, eg nothing but entering changes to employee records. This problem was most acute where staff had previously undertaken a wider range of tasks. For example, personnel assistants in small teams serving a single business unit had more variety than they have in shared service centres where they do a narrower range of tasks.

- by contrast, asking too much of the business facing HR managers in concentrating exclusively on strategy and change management, having removed their operational raison d'être. This has proved difficult for some HR managers, who felt the loss of power, whereas others have welcomed the chance to focus their work more on matters of greater significance.

- potential difficulties with future career development if lower graded staff do not build the expertise (possible in more generalist roles in traditional HR units) that allows them to fill more senior positions later.

- boundary management issues that occur where the service is heavily segmented, *eg* where does policy formation end and implementation begin?

- communication difficulties, again where there are numerous discrete activities, each organisationally separate. This is a perennial problem, with the interface with payroll seemingly the most difficult to get right.

- absence of effective accountability. HRMs may be responsible for the personnel services delivered to their business unit managers but have no control over the work if it is done in a shared service centre, managed by another HR team.

- lack of local knowledge. A feature in centralised shared services — personnel staff do not always know what is happening on the ground and are very reliant on being kept well informed.

- deciding to whom resources should be allocated, especially in a project organisation. The process should be more transparent than in the past, but the emphasis on prioritisation can leave individual business units dissatisfied with the result.

- the project based approach to functional support, which means that HR completes the task and moves on. In itself this is a good thing, ensuring that resources are well managed, but it can result in the consultant not seeing the work through to a real conclusion.

- the danger of creating project support that is ill-informed of business needs, *ie* is generic rather than specific in nature.

- too much emphasis on selling products, insufficient attention to the content.

- the loss of face-to-face contact, producing a depersonalised service. As a manager at Apple put it: '*My HR representative is not a person, it's a floppy disk*' (Eisenstat, 1996).

- large scale capital investment, which may be necessary to get the right technological infrastructure.

We will consider the bigger challenges to the shared services model that these and other issues raise, in Chapter 7.

6. The Future of Shared Services

6.1 Technological innovation

Most of the development in shared services is likely to come about through technological change. We can expect the use of intranets to become more widespread and sophisticated, with links into the Internet becoming commoner. In some companies this will align internal processes with external services of the e-commerce sort. Likewise, more business is likely to be done via the telephone, using call centres and helplines. More sophisticated computing power may be devoted to modelling systems, especially if flexible benefits really take off. Individuals are then able to model the impact of trading pay against holidays or extra pension provision against a bigger car. Mass customisation of terms and conditions is possible, as all variations and combinations can be recorded and monitored on the computer. Decision support mechanisms will allow managers to make better decisions on such things as discipline, training or selection. Proactive pull technology gets employees to think about the implications of changes in their personal circumstances. For example, if an employee notifies the system that they have got married, a prompt is generated asking if the beneficiary of death service provision should be adjusted.

This illustrates that the move to employee self service is becoming more practicable. Already line managers are being given on-line access to employee records, as yet with limited update rights. This is likely to be the stepping stone to managers authorising changes to pay or loading details on new recruits, authorised and actioned directly. Access to personal data might be extended to employees to allow them to alter their personal records. This may start with purely factual static data, but could become more sophisticated in relating to dynamic information, *eg* by encouraging employees to maintain training records, develop a skills inventory, express career development aspirations, compile a curriculum vitae and so on. Further developments could include interactive mechanisms, such as booking a training course. Cisco, an IT company, claims to have saved £30 million by automating HR administration, including applying employee self service (Whiteley, 1999).

Speed of progress will probably not be determined by technological capability, but by culture—how much is the organisation prepared to devolve responsibility to line managers or employees?—and by ease of access. In some organisations, nearly all employees have a desktop computer. Those that do not would be able through computer *kiosks* to get on-line. Kiosks or similar facilities naturally work best with a physically concentrated and stable workforce. It is more difficult to provide access to peripatetic workers who may rarely set foot in conventional offices. However, mobile communication equipment (*eg* via mobile phones) is likely to solve even this problem—albeit with a cost attached.

6.2 Organisational change

HR shared services may also change as organisational and customer needs alter. This may be to make use of the above technological innovation; to reduce costs still further by gaining greater economies of scale; to take account of the globalisation of business and internationalisation of resources. There may be specific drivers to change in particular locations. The birth of the EURO has generated consultancy activity predicated on an emerging harmonisation in reward structures across Europe that will best be supported by common shared service centres.

These pressures may be represented within organisations by extending the shared services concept to other parts of the business, subsidiaries or satellite companies. One case study organisation had implemented shared services within the principal business and was now considering extending it to other group companies. Organisations may seek cross-functional synergy in their service provision. Functional differences may be minimised as a common platform is used. HR, finance and logistics, for example, may use shared IT facilities and information to offer an integrated approach. This may offer the customer a single contact point for any administrative query, thereby making contact simpler for the customer. Shared services may also be offered round the clock to make it easier for those working non-standard hours to receive a service in their working time.

Nationally based service provision is already being replaced by cross-national operations — another reason for 24 hour opening is to allow communication with other shared service centres worldwide. Thus far, there does not seem to be an example of a *common* international offering; rather there seem to be regional centres which may be part of a single, international organisational structure. Hewlett Packard has a shared service centre for each continent. IBM is another example. It has a European HR service based in Portsmouth, handling phone calls and e-mails from managers and staff in a growing number of countries. It seems as if IBM has gone for a common service point so that language skills are the key capability of recruits. This is in contrast to HP where Didier Hirsch (European HR director) says:

> *'We changed the country based system, but allowed our managers to stay in the same offices. We send the work to the people, not the people to the work.'* (Rosenbaum, 1999)

Other arrangements might include supporting global business streams rather than organising on a geographic basis at the regional level.

There are, however, some limitations on what work can be done on a common, international basis. As Martin James of IBM says:

> *'Anything involving employment law is problematic. Anything to do with employee relations, works councils, procedures governing dismissal, how you set up a contract – all of these by definition are country focused.'* (Industrial Relations Services, 1999a)

Indeed, reward and benefits may also be locally determined, sometimes to reflect national law or practice. For some organisations, usually for the management cadre, there may be an attempt to reduce country differences and move to a common basis. ABN-AMRO, for example, have developed a common pay structure for their mobile, professional specialists.

Selling services externally may also become more common as the larger companies realise that they have expertise and capacity that can be utilised for the benefit of others. BT is about to do this in the UK; IBM has been doing the same in the USA for a few years.

Cross-organisation sharing of services might become more common, especially in the public sector. Reported in the literature is the example of six Lothian based NHS trusts that combined their HR services as a cost saving measure (Industrial Relations Services, 1998).

Outsourcing shared services to a third party provider can achieve similar economies of scale, as the supplier can offer services to a number of organisations from the same base. This is more likely to appeal to the small or medium sized companies that cannot afford the new interactive technology on their own.

One has to be careful about all the pronouncements on widespread outsourcing. Its growth has been much predicated but not yet delivered. For example, Mike Bett, former President of the IPD, said in 1994:

> 'There is an irreversible move, driven by information technology, towards the dispersal of all kinds of work away from the centre and out from the payroll. Many of the routine administrative things personnel departments do could be contracted out.'
> (quoted in Golzen, 1994)

The most up to date and comprehensive survey of organisations' HR behaviour, the Workplace Employee Relations Survey (WERS), found in 1998 that only one-quarter of organisations had contracted out work over the last five years. These tended to be the bigger organisations. Interestingly, 40 per cent of those outsourcing were in the non-commercial sector and one-third contracted out because of Compulsory Competitive Tendering. Of course, this means that the vast majority did not report any recent contracting out. Training (36 per cent) was much the most common HR activity to be undertaken externally. Payroll was outsourced by one-fifth of respondents and recruitment by only 11 per cent.

7. Issues in Creating Successful Shared Services

7.1 Challenges in getting it right

There are a number of different challenges that the shared services model poses to the way in which HR management is conducted in organisations.

7.1.1 Recognition of the value of administrative work

Organisations have the aspiration that by diminishing the importance of administrative activities, the HR function can concentrate on higher value added work. Whilst not always meaning to suggest that administrative work is of little consequence, respondents did talk of 'getting rid' of the transactional in a sort of 'out of sight, out of mind' way. There are two dangers in this approach. Administrative personnel work is vital to the smooth running of the operation of any organisation. If people are not paid on time or paid incorrectly, then there is understandable disgruntlement. Moreover, if employee records are a mess, not only are staff irritated, but any attempt to monitor employee patterns (*eg* the growth of part-time or temporary staff) is doomed to failure. One interviewee told me that there was no 'kudos' in administrative work. That may well be true, but the consequences of failure are high. As an American HR manager (quoted in Eisenstat, 1996) more graphically put it: *'Administration ... doesn't get you anything but a black eye if you screw it up.'*

It also makes HR vulnerable to the charge that if you cannot run a payroll successfully, how can you claim to be able to develop the competencies of staff or whatever.

The second consequence is that those HR staff working on administrative tasks see themselves as second class citizens doing jobs that are little regarded. This affects morale as well as recruitment to these posts. One case study organisation complained that getting quality staff to work on their helpline was handicapped by the fact that it was seen as a dumping ground for people who were not able to get a proper job elsewhere within the function. BOC found that they had to recruit most service centre staff from scratch because of the poor image of 'call centre' work (Turner, 2000).

7.1.2 Making the strategic contribution a reality

What of the other end of the spectrum: how does strategic positioning work? This is the goal for many HR organisations, but do they know what they are looking for? Do their business colleagues know how to include HR in strategic decision making and is this something they seek? Does the service culture make it harder to be successful in making a strategic contribution? And do HR staff have the skills to perform the role?

It is debatable how many organisations think through the strategic contribution they are expecting from their HR managers. Processes and content have to be considered, and agreed with managerial colleagues. It may be necessary to go to the root of what business strategy involves. There is a strong argument for not having separate functional strategies, but a single organisational one. This should have a people component, but the responsibility for determining it has to be decided. A partnership approach, whereby HR and management together consider and set the people related objectives of the organisation is an attractive one. It allows HR to bring its professional insight to bear, as well as management's knowledge of the business issues. However, it has been argued (Torrington, 1998 and Fowler, 1997) that the culture of purchaser/provider which is the basis of shared services, is antipathetic to HR developing a strategic role. The purchaser determines what will bought and the provider supplies it. There are, as Torrington says, echoes of master and servant in this relationship. It is not a partnership of equals of the sort that is necessary to develop a common strategy.

Some organisations feel that they have avoided this problem by restricting shared services to non-strategic matters, leaving the HR managers and corporate centre to concentrate on higher value added activities. This, though, requires some sophistication, as there are then multiple models in the HR and line management relationship. Different types of relationship — customer/supplier and strategic partner — apply at different points in the organisation.

Then there is the question of skills. There is a real question of whether HR managers, used to running an operational team, can suddenly successfully switch to being a strategic business partner. Previously, the HR manager has derived his/her power from ensuring smooth running of people related activities. Now the HR manager has to use a different set of skills that rely upon influencing without a resource or operational base, but through professional insight.

The HR manager in most of the shared services models we have described has become more like broker of services than a deliverer. This is because they have to call upon support from elsewhere. The shared services group carries out the administrative work. A project team is available to help with some form of change management activity. Centres of excellence can be used if specialist help is needed in, say, reward or performance management. So another skill required of the new HR manager is that of successfully co-ordinating the various players so that the business gets a coherent service.

7.1.3 Integrating HR

Segmenting HR services helps make clear to customers what they can expect from different parts of the function. Combining work into a shared service centre has advantages in resource optimisation and in improving learning within a particular team. There are, however, risks involved:

● The right hand does not know what the left hand is doing. So far from offering an integrated service, the line is presented with a disparate offering.

- Consultancy is given in a context free manner. In other words, because those in the consultancy pool have no particular knowledge of any business, they give generalised rather than tailored advice. This may mean that local issues are ignored. *'Many of the consultants find they've been detached from the business, they're pulled in to do a consulting job, and then sent away again.'* (Hutchinson and Wood, 1995)

- Some personnel staff become detached from the business. They provide services to it but in an indirect manner — they lack the feel of what is going on in the business and lack commitment to it.

- There is poor organisational learning across groups. Problems which are identified in one area are not picked up elsewhere. Thus, those handling the administration of relocation may be aware of individual difficulties that policy makers should know. Helplines may discover a series of disputes in the same business unit that centre on a particular manager, but, as they are organisationally divorced from the problem, they have to convince others of the importance of the issue.

- Boundary disputes occur over who is responsible for what. Those charged with implementing policy complain that they are given insufficient guidance and have themselves to flesh out policies. Helplines pass problems to others if they become too complicated, but specialists may believe that insufficient is being done in escalating only the really difficult cases.

Of course, many of these issues can be tackled by training (ensuring people know their jobs and what others are doing); by putting a high premium on communication both internally within teams but also across them; and by organisation (some companies have aligned their project teams or administrative functions so that they handle the work of specific business units and thereby build up local knowledge).

7.1.4 Efficiency versus choice in customer service

Another set of issues concerns customer service. If the shared services concept is distinguished by the fact that it is customer focused, what type and nature of services will the customer want? Tensions have already arisen in some of our case study organisations. Line managers have persuaded HR to return to involvement in recruitment activities despite HR's attempts at withdrawing from this work in a spirit of devolvement.

Supporters of shared services say that this is not a problem so long as the customer is prepared to pay. But the philosophical underpinning of devolvement is about line managers accepting their responsibilities, not finding a paid mercenary.

What if the customer wants to challenge more fundamental tenets of people management? Is the customer always right? Here there is a tension between whether HR is merely giving advice which the line manager can accept or reject, or whether the HR function is guardian of corporate values or principles. If it is a matter of the manager wanting to break the law, maybe the issue is clear cut, but what if the manager is going against good practice? Should HR challenge and in what way? As one HR manager put it, there is a fear of *'sacrificing professional standards for operational expediency'* (Hall and Torrington, 1998).

Then there are the questions of whether corporate efficiency has a higher value than customer specificity. To give an example quoted to me: should an organisation have numerous redundancy compensation schemes for different groups or sites, or have a common approach? The former is easy to manage, and defend against accusations of favouritism, but the latter can be better tailored to occupational or local circumstances — *ie* be better market attuned. So HR has to decide whether policies should be treated as commodities, where the lowest delivery price should be sought, or whether they are bespoke items attuned to business need.

Having SLAs with money attached sharpens the debate. If it is true that things that are measured get attention, there is a danger of distortion in the services provided, unless the SLA is very comprehensive. HR staff have targets to meet and these are the matters that get dealt with. Other matters not covered by the SLA get ignored. This suggests that longer term or more complex change issues get sidelined. For example, HR might be convinced that equal opportunities training is needed, given evidence of discrimination in recruitment or promotion selection. The line may accord this a low priority and not be prepared to pay for it. Moreover, there is the pressure to deliver what the customer says they want, or to focus most on sympathetic managers, not necessarily the ones who need the most help. As Russell Eisenstat reports on some American research:

'Many members who worked under a charge-back system were concerned that there was pressure on them to move away from a consideration of what was right for the corporation as a whole and toward a greater concern with how they could sell enough services to cover their expenses.' (Eisenstat, 1996)

These are not new issues but they do become more pertinent in a customer driven world.

7.1.5 Will the centralisation pendulum swing back?

Proponents of shared services say that this question is no longer relevant because the structure now meets the customer's needs, be it through centrally or dispersed provision. In fact, it is still a relevant question. Shared services are predicated on the benefits of having a common approach to save money and improve standards. It offers consistency of operation. But what of autonomy? What if one business wants its recruitment done one way, not the standard way, or it wants its records held differently? If the customer can choose what they can have, then consistency and standardisation are sacrificed in favour of free choice. It was on this basis that all the multiplicity of payroll and record systems were allowed in organisations in the 1980s. Having a common system merely reverts back to the earlier days of centralisation!

Some organisations have faced the issue head on. They have distinguished between those services that are common, as determined by corporate fiat (payroll and records), from those which are optional (recruitment, relocation *etc.*) where the business unit can take the corporate service, do it themselves or buy from elsewhere. There is still the difficulty that those wanting a common service might have different ideas on what it means. One business unit might want a high volume recruitment service with little sophistication, whereas another business unit might want tailor-made recruitment with intensive contact with each candidate. Services can of course be adjusted to do both, but it does leave the service provider in a position of having to juggle to meet customer needs. As one manager complained, all the effort goes into defining and pricing the service rather than into establishing that it serves the right organisational purpose.

7.1.6 HR's role with respect to employees

We have assumed thus far that the customers are the line managers, and probably rightly so. But do employees have a position as customers? In some HR organisations, the impression is given that employees are incidental to the function's work. This is because the desire for strategic alignment with the business suggests that HR is interested in management perspectives, not those of the employee. HR is so keen to remove the employee welfare tag that it strives to emphasise its links with managers, whilst cutting them from employees. This is not to say that employees are entirely neglected. Counselling services have been introduced, but provided through an outsourced supplier, detached from the HR function. Intranets or helplines may be used by employees. Yet the thrust of HR's realignment is to become as one with other business colleagues.

Is this right? Naturally, it depends upon where HR wishes to position itself. But even if HR's aspiration is to be a strategic partner, what is it that makes the HR contribution distinctive? If it has no special expertise, what right has it to sit alongside finance, marketing or production? The answer is that HR's expertise is in its knowledge of people—what makes them tick, what motivates them to contribute to organisational performance, what inclines them to stay or leave the organisation, *etc.* HR has also played the role of managing the employment relationship, handling '*the inherent tension and conflict between the imperatives of the market, the organisational demands for control of employees, and the individual needs of people at work*' (Keenoy, 1989).

If this is HR's area of knowledge, how will this be maintained in some of these new structures? HR managers in the business units will need to work hard to establish people problems without the benefit of having the eyes and ears of the rest of their team. Attitude surveys become important, as do satisfaction surveys of HR services. But some organisations concentrate exclusively on line managers and their views on service. The argument is that they pay for the HR activities. This may neglect the real end-customer who has experienced the service, be it a training course, relocation or maternity absence.

These issues of getting a feel for the organisational temperature can be exacerbated where there is little face to face contact with managers or employees. Instead, impersonal media like computers or telephones dominate. Where employees are widely dispersed in small units, this may be understandable. Indeed, there may be more contact with HR in this way than in the past, but there is less reason in large offices or factories. One case study organisation felt this to be a sufficiently important matter that they deliberately sited their shared services centre in a prominent position and inducted all new starters within the same room so that they would know where it was.

If de-personalisation does occur, there are risks to organisational efficiency — people treat their colleagues as names and numbers not people, in a way that threatens co-operative teamworking. There are potential problems too for HR staff who may, as Ulrich rightly observed, have entered the profession because they liked people. They may become quickly disillusioned if they discover that instead they face a computer screen all day.

7.1.7 Devolvement or dumping?

We have identified earlier that the devolution of activities from HR to the line has been a common theme in people management in recent years. The introduction of shared services has taken place within this context. HR's desire to become more strategic, and the HRM philosophy to make managers responsible for people management, have given impetus to devolution. Research, however, suggests some organisations have devolved activities by dumping work on the line managers with insufficient training and support, and inadequate resources to complete the work. This may cause minor difficulties or more serious concerns, such as the potential for racism in conducting disciplinary or performance management cases (Rick *et al.*, 1999). Moreover, it cannot be assumed that managers have had their views sought on devolution. Indeed, in research done in 1994, a significant minority, over one-third of organisations, had not consulted managers before devolving work to them (Industrial Relations Services, 1994).

This is an issue in the introduction of shared services. In considering who should complete activities, HR has been trying to free itself from mundane work. It has often sought to pass these tasks to line managers to do — to record information, to run processes like sickness absence. Some tasks transferred to the line may be of higher value — for example, managing performance related pay reviews, interviewing for recruitment or conducting performance management processes. If the work is mundane, line managers may query why they should be expected to do the work. Or, if they do not quibble in this way and are able to find resources to do the work, they create new armies of clerks, thereby reducing the overall organisational cost efficiency.

If the work is more complex, there is the question of whether managers have the competence to perform the tasks. In the past, this has been a reason why HR has resisted devolvement—a good idea in theory, but not in practice, given the skills of the managers. Yet, trying to get the line to realise their responsibilities in people management, leads organisations inevitably towards devolvement. The question is then: how well will devolution be implemented? Will managers be selected with account taken of their people management skills, as well as their technical know-how? Will their performance be appraised on the basis of their team management or merely on meeting their sales or output target? Will the managers be adequately trained in recruitment, performance management, reward or whatever areas of responsibility they now have? Will HR be available to give guidance and practical support to managers in the execution of their duties? And finally will line managers be given adequate time to perform their personnel role? Pressures on managers to get the job done, with inadequate resources and with little reward for any people management efforts, have been reported as the principal constraints on successful devolution in practice (McGovern *et al.*, 1997).

Another part of HRM thinking—that managers should exercise their right to manage—has also made devolution more problematic for HR managers. How do we give the line greater authority for people management and yet ensure they exercise their responsibilities in such a way that does not harm the organisation overall? The ambiguity of HR's position is apparent. It seeks to facilitate change, and perform the role of adviser to the line manager, but yet it finds it difficult to stop adopting a policing role. It seems hard for HR to avoid being '*props and cops*' (an American manager quoted in Eisenstat, 1996) supporting the line to solve its problems and acting as the corporate enforcer to prevent managers breaking the rules.

Getting this wrong may have serious consequences. There is the report of a personnel director having to rein back on managers' responsibilities when he discovered that there were sixteen employment tribunal cases running concurrently (Hutchinson and Wood, 1995). Managers may not exercise their responsibilities in line with corporate needs — seen, for example, in how performance management processes are handled. They may exhibit behaviour that is not in line with organisational values, say in relation to minority groups.

What does HR then do? Probably all HR staff accept the primacy of the relationship between the manager and his/her own staff. HR members would not wish to interfere with how this relationship is managed. And yet, HR would be concerned if managers break the rules, and if it sees itself as the employee champion, would HR step in if they are being unreasonably treated? Again this pushes HR back to being a policeman and to involving itself in the way managers exercise their people-related duties.

7.1.8 Getting the design right

There are several choices to be made in the way in which shared services are delivered. The most crucial is whether to 'make or buy', *ie* whether to perform tasks internally or externally. There are various decision making models available (Reilly and Tamkin, 1997) to help organisations make their choice. Figure 5 is a simple schematic that addresses both devolvement and outsourcing.

Figure 5: Issues to be considered in devolvement and outsourcing

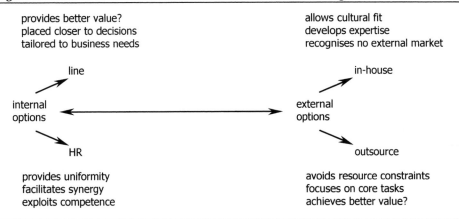

Source: IES, adapted from Flood et al. (1995)

Most organisations will contemplate market testing aspects of their personnel function to see whether outsourcing is an appropriate route to take. Very few, if any, organisations would contemplate outsourcing the whole HR activity. The corporate role in particular, with its emphasis on strategy and governance would normally remain in-house, as would those activities where organisational knowledge is especially vital.

Simply put, on the one hand, the benefits of contracting parts of the HR function are to:

- save costs
- switch from *fixed* to *variable* costs
- improve service by use of use of a specialist supplier
- free up managerial time to focus on core business issues
- give greater flexibility in meeting fluctuating work demand
- reduce exposure to regulations, legislation *etc.*
- reduce headcount (if not necessarily costs).

On the other hand, there are reported problems associated with outsourcing:

- contractual (legal) difficulties
- service problems
- lack of expertise to manage contractors
- employee relations issues, *eg* over the terms of the transfer, selection, consultation and negotiation
- unexpected costs
- the presence of a new bureaucracy to monitor contractor performance
- the inability of managers to adjust, or the absence of the necessary skills
- poor communication between contractor and client.

Some of these issues can be dealt with by careful attention to the process of transition and are likely to be only short term in nature. However, some commentators and managers believe there are the more profound risks that stem from losing control over an activity, especially where there is a fundamental difference of outlook between the contractor (wishing to maximise profit) and the client (aiming to minimise cost). Again,

The Institute for Employment Studies

organisations have felt they have circumvented this problem by entering a *partnership deal* with their supplier. This emphasises the mutuality of the relationship—the fact that both parties are reliant on each other for success, and risks and rewards are shared.

Those organisations contemplating outsourcing seem to have to choose between a partnership relationship (especially with complex or important services) or to enter a purely transactional deal, but restrict it to services that are relatively easy to define and manage.

There are those organisations that believe, almost as a matter of principle, that better cost and/or service can be provided in house. If this is the case, then there are still decisions to be made. Do you set up an internal subsidiary company to provide shared services? Do you instead create a separate profit centre, or merely cost centre? More conventionally, are shared services integrated into the normal work of the HR department? The outcome of your thinking is likely to be affected by whether you intend to:

- sell your services externally
- offer them to other parts of the business, *eg* internationally
- create SLAs with your business partners
- count HR costs as part of a corporate overhead.

Those answering 'yes' at the top of the list are likely at least to create separate cost centres, whilst those treating HR costs as an overhead are unlikely to see the worth of a discreet business within the function.

Having decided whether to outsource or insource, there is then the question of staffing levels. Some organisations seem to be bewitched by benchmarking. They believe that by seeing what others do, they get a profound insight into what they should do. If there is a genuine like for like comparison, then this may be possible. Unfortunately, it rarely is the case. What is included in HR varies from organisation to organisation. Even if the HR units can be shaped to make a fair comparison, the business needs are unlikely to be the same. Benchmarking has its place in testing numbers and examining processes in the light of others' experience. Reductionist use of ratios to determine your staffing levels seems misconceived. It does not give sufficient attention to the quality of the service or the needs of the customers.

7.1.9 Technological traumas

One challenge faced by a number of the case study organisations was that they suffered from over-expectations of the speed and nature of technological improvement. This might simply have been an over-ambitious timetable for their implementation project. If it merely meant delay, the difficulty was easier to cope with than changes taking place elsewhere in the organisation, on the assumption that systems and software had altered, when this was not the case. One organisation suffered grievously from this problem. They made staffing changes on the supposition that the IT kit was going to be in place. The result was that the quality of the service was poor and this meant that the shared service centre got off to a bad start, allowing critics to rubbish the new concept.

Another difficulty reported by several organisations was that some of the supposed time saving technology did not deliver. Either systems crashed, did not work, or did not do what they were supposed to do. This might be because of fundamental flaws in the system design, or, more likely, due to problems in the way the system was set up. Again, if staffing was predicated on time savings, *eg* from using computer text scanning that did not materialise, then services might suffer. Alternatively, the benefits of technology might not be seen. For example, having data on computer allows it to be shared among a number of users. If the technology fails, line managers or different HR teams may be denied access to vital information.

The lesson is that organisations must be cautious in project management and in the selection of computer products. The first may be easier than the second to accomplish. Computer sales people can be very persuasive. HR may be pushed by other parts of the organisation towards choosing particular solutions. The risk is that, as one interviewee complained, you end up with unsuitable technology that does not deliver what you want either now or in the future.

7.1.10 Getting senior management backing

Conference Board research discovered that more than half of the organisations responding to an American survey, felt that the transformation of HR was foundering on a lack of articulated vision of where HR should re-position itself or by the lack of senior management support for change (Brenner, 1996). Several organisations in the Hutchinson and Wood study for the IPD (1995) also reported a lack of top management support for changing the role of HR and especially devolving responsibilities to line managers.

In our study, a number of organisations stressed the importance of getting early buy-in to change from senior management. This may be necessary to ensure that there is support against those resisting organisational innovation.

7.2 Responding to the challenges

7.2.1 The current position

If one makes a critical appraisal of where the shared services concept stands on the basis of research that has been done, the result, set out in terms of Ulrich's model of HR's future role (1998), might be as shown in Figure 6.

Some organisations have undoubtedly improved their administrative services, but there is a danger of getting into a state of mind that sees these activities as unimportant and disposable, because of the search for higher value added work. Yet, whether the HR function likes it or not, it is frequently judged on its

Figure 6: Ulrich's role model for HR: a critical appraisal of current status

partner in strategy   *aspirational*   change agent

questionable   *marginalised?*

employee champion   administrative expert

Source: Adapted from Ulrich (1998)

capacity to do the basics right. And this applies to senior managers as much as to shop floor workers.

Similarly, in the desire to be aligned with the business, some organisations either deny the employee champion role or relegate it to a purely care and maintenance state — keeping the employees quiet being the primary concern. This feeling is supported by research in both the UK (Poole and Jenkins, 1996) and America (Conference Board work reported in Brenner, 1996) which suggests that HR's emphasis is more on business alignment than on being an employee advocate. The result may be that HR is not equipped either to represent employee interests or to make clear how employees will respond to business initiatives. This may make HR remote to employees and thereby less effective in facilitating cultural change (Cunningham and Hyman, 1999). There is the tension, alluded to earlier in this chapter, between HR conforming to the dominant values of the organisation in practice or challenging them (Legge, 1978). This issue applies both to whether being a service provider ensures that the former is the norm, and to the employee advocate role where challenge is more likely to take place.

The same may be said about the strategic contribution HR aims to make. The function may have a long way to go before it can consider itself successful. Research suggests that change in organisations has more often been caused by downsizing than by a drive for strategic re-alignment (Connolly, *et al.*, 1997). This has been compounded by a failure of HR to define and secure its re-positioning. As Cunningham and Hyman argue, there is an optimistic scenario that HR does indeed become a strategic player, and the introduction of shared services could facilitate this. But there is the pessimistic possibility that HR itself becomes marginalised, unable to act strategically and without responsibility for activities devolved to the line, outsourced or transferred elsewhere.

7.2.2 Criteria for success

So what steps can HR management take to improve the chances of success? Here are some ideas:

● Recognise that HR has a number of different customers (*eg* senior management who determine policy direction, line managers who may purchase services, employees who will consume services, their representatives, external bodies, *etc.*) with different needs. Do not pretend that in satisfying one customer (*eg* the line manager) you have satisfied them all.

- It is poor psychology to tell your customers what is best for them. It is better to agree what your services will be and what they key deliverables are—in this way the shared services concept is spot on. This may mean standardising some activities, whilst giving others getting scope for more customisation.

- Spend some time seeing how your HR processes fit together. Without necessarily going the whole hog of completing a Business Process Re-engineering exercise, re-configure HR to fit with the outputs to the customer. Do not get stuck with structures routed in history or ones that fit the producer's rather than the consumer's needs.

- Find the most effective and efficient means of delivering quality services. This might be through a shared service centre, line managers or local HR managers. Be pragmatic not dogmatic as to which is the best route for the particular service. (Figure 7 may help stimulate this sort of decision making.)

- Be equally pragmatic about whether activities should be kept in-house or outsourced. Decide on a cost/benefit basis over the long term as well as the short term, making sure that quality considerations are given as much emphasis as financial ones.

- Give high level attention to the monitoring of services. Specify the key clients and obtain credible measures of whether you are meeting their needs. You should aim for the virtuous circle outlined in Figure 8, that sees service delivery as an integrated activity from start to finish.

- Work hard on skilling the HR managers so that they can make a full contribution to meeting local business unit needs, at the strategic or operational level.

- Devolve responsibilities and proper authority to line managers in appropriate areas, but ensure they have positive support from their HR colleagues.

- Ensure that your customers understand under what principles and values you are operating. Specify which policies are sacrosanct and not open to challenge. In other words, spell out HR's governance function.

- Be clear as to the roles of the various HR players. Recognise that there will be overlaps, but insist on maximum communication to keep all parties well informed. Specify escalation procedures clearly.

Figure 7: Decision tree on who should execute HR activities

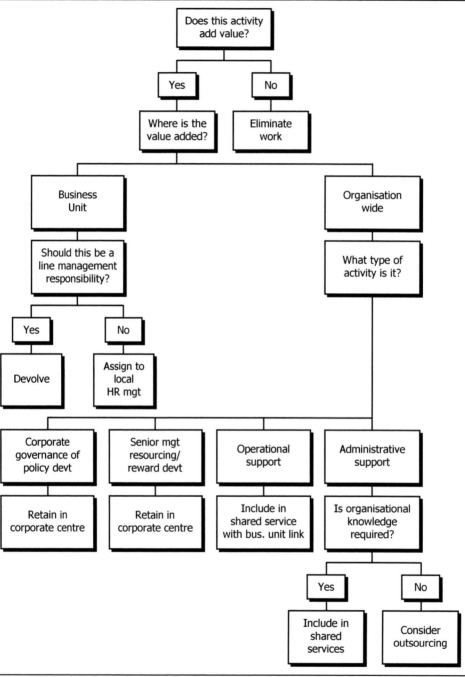

Source: *Adapted from Lentz (1996)*

The Institute for Employment Studies

Figure 8: Getting the right service provision

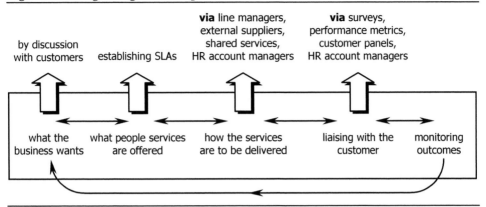

Source: IES

- Understand that there will be boring, repetitive activities to be undertaken within a shared service centre. Either automate them out or ensure that through task rotation people have a variety of things to do.

- Recognise the importance of local knowledge of the culture of particular business unit, of the issues facing that department or the characteristics of the boss. This can be done by aligning HR activities to support specific business units.

- Whilst making use of communication technology to keep a disparate team well informed and able to access common data, aim for the highest possible co-location of staff, primarily for reasons of maximising the chances of sharing and learning.

- Broaden the know-how of your staff and improve teamwork by rotating people through different jobs as much as is possible, whilst ensuring a professional service is maintained and accepting that there are differences in capabilities between individuals.

- Encourage the development of line manager access and employee self service in data management. This should improve the involvement of managers in personnel work and give a greater sense of ownership to employees, of their personal information, making it more likely that it will be better maintained.

- Whilst trying to encourage employees to use the cheapest media, understand that different access routes suit people in different situations. Telephone contact may be easiest for home or mobile workers, whereas the intranet may be better for those in the office. In setting access routes, be aware of the disadvantages of impersonal media. Recognise that in some circumstances face to face contact may be desirable.

7.2.3 Changing context

There is cause to be optimistic regarding HR's attempt to re-position itself; there have been a number of recent developments in the external environment that might help:

● the election of a Labour government that, by comparison with its Conservative predecessors, is more interventionist (*eg* on the Minimum Wage), more accepting of the EU employment agenda (*eg* Working Time Regulations or Social Chapter), more concerned with maximising the labour supply (the family friendly agenda or New Deal) and prepared to re-legislate on employee relations (*eg* new trade union recognition rules).

● a tighter labour market, making recruitment more difficult and placing greater emphasis on retention measures, especially on reward and recognition.

● an environment of partnership in employee relations between trade unions and employers, resulting in some specific deals, for example, exchanging employee acceptance of change for reassurances on job security.

● a growing body of research that shows the positive impact of good people policies on bottom line performance, and a changing intellectual climate that talks more about the competitive advantage to be derived from organisational capability and less about market positioning.

These developments put HR to the fore. Whether the function can benefit depends a lot on how well its attempt at re-positioning itself works. As we have seen, introducing shared services could be an element in this process, along with devolvement, but this route is not without its challenges. If these are successfully met, then HR may succeed in defining a new agenda for itself.

8. References

Adams K (1991), 'Externalisation Versus Specialisation: What is Happening to Personnel?', *HRM Journal*, Vol. 1, No. 4, pp. 40-54

Arkin A (1999), 'Return to Centre', *People Management*, 6 May p. 34

Brenner L (1996), 'The Disappearing HR Department', *CFO Publishing Corp*, Vol. 12, No. 3

Connolly T R, Mardis W, Down J W (1997), 'Transforming Human Resources', *Management Review*, Vol. 86, No. 6, pp. 10-16

Cunningham I, Hyman J (1999), 'Devolving Human Resource Responsibilities to the Line', *Personnel Review*, Vol. 28, No. 1-2, pp. 9-27

Dierdorff C (1996), 'Improving Effectiveness of Human Resources Services', *The Public Manager*, Vol. 25, No. 3, pp. 45-47

Eisenstat R A (1996), 'What Corporate Human Resources Brings to the Picnic: Four Models for Functional Management', *Organizational Dynamics*, Vol. 25, No. 2, pp. 6-14

Flood P C, Gannon M J, Pauwe J (1995), *Managing Without Traditional Methods: International Innovations in HRM*, Addison and Wesley

Fowler A (1997), 'How to Outsource Personnel', *People Management*, 20 February

Golzen G (1994), 'Views From the Top', *Human Resources*, Spring, pp. 29, 30, 32

Hall L, Torrington D (1998), 'Letting go or Holding on—the Devolution of Operational Personnel Activities', *Human Resource Management Journal*, Vol. 8, No. 1

Hammond D (1999), 'BT Answers Business Call for HR Outsourcing Service', *Personnel Today*, 23 September

Hirschfield R (1996), 'Shared Services Save Big Money', *Datamation*

Hirschfield R (1994), 'The Centre Cannot Hold: Devolving Personnel Duties', *IRS Employment Trends*, No. 566

Hirschfield R, Currie C (1997), 'Shared Service Centres and Employee Self-service: Concepts are often confused, but not confusing', *Employee Benefit Plan Review*, Vol. 51, No. 8

Holbeche L (1998), 'Too Close to the Client?', *People Management*, 24 December

Hoogendoorn J, Brewster C (1992), 'Human Resource Aspects: Decentralization and Devolution', *Personnel Review*, Vol. 21, No. 1, pp. 4-11, MCB University Press

Hutchinson S, Wood S (1995), 'The UK Experience', in *Personnel and the Line: Developing the New Relationship*, Institute of Personnel Development

Industrial Relations Services (1999a), 'IBM Delivers International HR,' October, *Employment Trends*, No. 689

Industrial Relations Services (1999b), 'Privatising Personnel,' July, *Employment Trends*, No. 684

Industrial Relations Services (1998), *The Evolving HR Function*, Issue 10, July

Industrial Relations Services (1994), 'The Centre Cannot Hold: Devolving Personnel Duties,' *Employment Trends*, No. 566

Kessler I, Coyle-Shapiro J, Purcell J 'Outsourcing and the Employee Perspective', *Human Resource Management Journal*, Vol. 9, No. 2

Keenoy T (1989), 'HRM: A Case of the Wolf in Sheep's Clothing?', *Personnel Review*, Vol. 19, No. 2

Lapointe J R (1997), 'A Method for Selecting the Right Employee Self-service Solution', *Human Resource Management*, Vol. 42, No. 8, pp. 37-42

Lecky-Thompson R (1997), 'Tales of the City', *Personnel Management*, January, pp. 22-27

Legge K (1978), *Power, Innovation and Problem Solving in Personnel Management*, McGraw-Hill

Lentz S S (1996), 'Hybrid Organization Structures: A Path to Cost Savings and Customer Responsiveness', *Human Resource Management,* Vol. 35, No. 4, pp. 453-469

Merrick N (1999), 'Premier Division', *People Management,* 19 August

McGovern P, Gratton L, Hope-Hailey V, Stiles P, Truss C (1997), 'Human Resource Management on the Line?', *Human Resource Management Journal,* Vol. 7, No. 4

McWilliams B S (1996), 'Have you Considered Insourcing?' *Across the Board,* Vol. 33, No. 10, pp. 31-34

Overell S (1999), 'Of conflict', *Personnel Today,* 10 June

Pickard J (2000), 'The Truth is Out There', *People Management,* 3 February

Poole M, Jenkins G (1996), *Back to the Line? A Survey of Managers' Attitudes to Human Resource Management,* London Institute of Management

Purcell J, Ahlstrand B (1994), *Human Resource Management in Multi-Division Companies,* OUP

Reilly P, Tamkin P (1997), *Outsourcing: a Flexible Option for the Future?,* Institute for Employment Studies, Report 320

Reilly P (1996), *Human Resource Planning: An Introduction,* Institute for Employment Studies, Report 312

Rick J, Tamkin P, Tackey N, Pollard E (2000), *Institutional Racism: Where's the Prejudice in Organisations?,* Paper presented to the British Psychological Society Occupational Psychology Conference, Brighton, January

Rosenbaum A (1999), 'Back Offices and the Euro', *Human Resources,* June

Smethurst S, Kimber A (1999), 'In Pursuit of Lean HR,' *Human Resources,* September

Thatcher M (1996), 'A Platform for Sharing', *People Management,* 30 May

Thornhill A, Saunders M (1998), 'What if line managers don't realize they're responsible for HR?', *Personnel Review,* Vol. 27, No. 6, pp. 460-476

Torrington D (1998), 'Crisis and Opportunity in HRM: the Challenge for the Personnel Function', in Sparrow P, Marchington M (eds), *Human Resource Management: The New Agenda,* London: Pitman Financial Times

Torrington D (1989), 'Human Resource Management and the Personnel Function', in Storey J (ed.), *New Perspectives on Human Resource Management*, Routledge

Turner A (2000), 'Central Preservation', *People Management*, March

Ulrich D (1995), 'Shared Services: From Vogue to Value', *Human Resource Planning*, Vol. 18, (3), pp. 12-23

Ulrich D (1997), 'Human Resource Champions: The Next Agenda for Adding Value and Delivering Results', *Harvard Business School Press*

Ulrich D (1998a), 'HR with Attitude', *People Management*, 13 August, pp. 36-39

Ulrich D (1998b), 'A New Mandate for Human Resources', *Harvard Business Review*, January-February

Whiteley P (1999), 'IT Giant Saves £30m by Automating HR Admin', *Personnel Today*, 15 April

Wilkinson A, Marchington M (1994), 'TQM: Instant Pudding for the Personnel Function?', *Human Resource Management Journal*, Vol. 5, No. 1, pp. 33-49